T0158689

# TOKENS IN AN INDIAN GRAVEYARD

Books by Linda Hussa

*Diary of a Cow Camp Cook:*
*or Buckaroos Around a Campfire Beats a Full House*
*Where the Wind Lives: Poems from the Great Basin*
*Ride the Silence*
*Lige Langston: Sweet Iron*
*Blood Sister, I Am to These Fields*
*Sharing Fencelines:*
*Three Friends Write from Nevada's Sagebrush Corner*

Edited

*Phil Stadtler: I Made A Lot of Tracks*

# Tokens in an Indian Graveyard

## Poems and Stories of Northern Paiute People

## Linda Hussa

Rainshadow Editions
The Black Rock Press
University of Nevada, Reno
2008

ISBN 978-1-891033-37-7

Library of Congress Control Number: 2007942997

Printed in the United States of America

The Black Rock Press
University of Nevada, Reno Reno, NV 89557-0044
www.blackrockpress.org

First Edition


Acknowledgements:

"The Fort Bidwell Indian School" was published
in the *Journal of the Modoc County Historical Society*,
No. 12 – 1990.

Some poems have been previously
published in other forms.

*To these people of Surprise Valley*
*And, always, to John*

# Contents

# Foreword

These stories and poems happened or were told to me the way we pass on all important information—by having enthusiasm for a story. Sometimes we can even recall how the day was when it happened, or how happy it made us feel to hear the story, or how sad, and how we began immediately making it our own, that is what I've written here, stories, so we do not forget.

It is not meant to be an ethnographic study of the Northern Paiute People, but they and the places are real and revered by many generations. Harsh and unkind things have been said or done by both races. It is not my aim to stir those feelings but to remember that all human beings have the capacity to forgive. How else could we continue on?

Tokens are around us every minute of our lives, connections to people here and gone, memories to ground us, and fulfill us. Tokens help us to understand we must participate fully. It is our duty. It is our gift.

I wish to thank Bob Blesse, director of The Black Rock Press and designer of this book; Catherine S. Fowler for her gracious assistance, Marilyn Livingston for her careful read, Carole Fisher, my friend who, if there were notes on these pages, could sing us the opera of these many lifetimes; John for leading me into this place, and to those who let me find how I could also belong here.

## Surprise Valley and the Desert Beyond

THE WESTERN LIP OF THE GREAT BASIN turns up in the Warner Mountains, forming a boundary Northern Paiute bands rarely crossed. The topography of the desert rolling eastward to the Wasatch is often linked in people's minds to a kind of outback, for good reason. It is a forbidding land of extreme temperatures and few resources to sustain life. Unless it is your homeland. If the horizon gives you comfort, if you know in which quarter of the sky the sun and moon will rise, if water sings you to its seep, seeds fill your basket, antelope can be charmed to your purpose, then you are satisfied.

I married John Hussa in 1971 and came to Surprise Valley knowing nothing of the native people, never having stood in their presence. In the world of my childhood, conformity was the rule. People hoped for country club invitations and waited with interest for the showroom unveiling of new cars every fall. Anthill cities called workers in. Clocks ticked on every wall, watches on every arm, no one took notice of those who stood beside them on the bus every morning. There was little room for deviation. Paychecks were the ruler you stood tall for.

Surprise Valley was the home I needed, open land in every direction, people working with cattle and horses, serving their community as family. Although I married a man, the ceremony should have included these vows:

> Do you take this valley,
> all the people in it
> good neighbors and bad,
> and the desert beyond,
> in drought or in plenty,
> until in eternity
> you and it
> join?

The desert under my feet was only just beginning to lap up over the soles of my boots. The process is as slow as the trickle of water through rock, if you stand still for it. And I was yet to meet a person of the Northern Paiute tribe, only one generation from their free wandering days.

A truck drove up our ranch road while I was working in the barn. A man with long, loose black hair leaned against his truck stopped in front of our house. Longhaired men were on the news each night, of a kind that held onto the acid '60s. This man was not like that. As I walked toward him he held out a long silver fish, iron gray over the back, spotted randomly, a scarlet slash at the throat. Steady eyes held no expression of greeting. Did I want to buy it?

Not knowing what was the right thing, I said no.

He turned, slid the fish back into a cooler in the bed of his truck, and drove out.

The Lahontan Cutthroat trout swam the waters of ancient Lake Lahontan, the dominant feature of western Nevada 75,000 years ago. Climatic changes that dried up layers of time and sent it flying on the winds into oblivion drew the lake in, shrinking Lahontan down to nine smaller lakes.

Native people expanded into the land left vacant by the receding shoreline of Lake Lahontan, living for thousands of years by hunting animals and birds, fishing, and harvesting the nuts, tubers and the frail seed plants of the arid lands. The Lahontan Cutthroat trout of those remnant lakes was a major food source for the Northern Paiute People.

In the 1840s, the white migration brought a devastating change to the Great Basin. The scarcity of food forced the Paiute people to live a nomadic life, traveling in small family bands that rarely settled for any period of time. They had no strength of numbers to launch an organized resistance against the force of whites, and they succumbed to their bitter destiny. A U.S. Army post was established at Fort Bidwell at the northern end of Surprise Valley to protect the white settlers. When the post closed in 1901, the compound was converted into an Indian school.

An unnatural force drove the Paiutes from their nomadic tradition and culture; Lake Lahontan's dominance over the landscape was diminished by climate long ago; both were reduced to a shadow of their original power by forces outside their control. Yet, they remain connected. Summit Lake in Nevada is the nearest remnant of Lake Lahontan to Surprise Valley. Management of its Lahontan Cutthroat trout fishery falls to Paiute families who live on the reservation land that follows the shoreline of Summit Lake.

John's mother Kay bought fish from the Summit Lake men who caught them and milked them and carried them more than one-hundred miles in coolers to sell to Surprise Valley ranchers they knew. She was a regular on their list. I was not.

The fish, fat with spring insects, held out in those two brown hands like an offering of friendship, was the only Lahontan Cutthroat trout I have ever seen.

In the early 1970s, the Modoc County Historical Society launched a project to collect oral histories of pioneer families. The organization of citizen-historians recognized the loss to society and community with every pioneer funeral. I saw it as a chance to meet my neighbors in a formal setting, to learn their history and, therefore, the histories of California, Nevada, and Oregon, the states whose corners touch a few miles to the northeast.

Cups of coffee set out for a visitor were a symbol of something important happening. Across kitchen tables, ranchers and their wives taught me the value and difficulty of their lives.

An elderly women told me that when she was seventeen, her husband left her in the late stage of pregnancy to join the fall gather of their cattle. Her only companion, her kid brother, was told to ride for help if she started into labor. One morning she felt her baby coming. But she was afraid to be alone and would not let the boy go for help. She forced herself to pretend bravery and calmly directed him as he birthed her first child.

Another woman took a yard rake out to the desert and raked the wool off a band of sheep that had frozen to death in a freak spring storm. She wove the wool into rugs and gave them to people in the valley to keep their feet warm while they dressed in the dark for work.

A man stood straight as a young sapling, looking into the summer sky and told me how he stood on that very spot one morning with his mother, his brother, and his aunt as the ash of Mount Lassen's eruption fell at his feet.

Another told of soldiers on a winter raid of a Paiute camp. When the killing was done, they snatched children and tied them on their backs as protection from a freezing north wind. When they reached the fort, they discarded the babies as they would throw down an empty feed sack.

John's childhood friendships led me into the Paiute community. Their unflinching stories told us all how they endured the wrongs they suffered at the hands of the white teachers and constable, of some ranchers and their wives, while others treated them with friendship and kindness. They defined their lives around a world changed, and lived hoping to lead their children forward without losing the past.

Initially, Nellie Townsend was reserved in my company, having been asked too many times to share her wisdom. But she softened when I asked of her acquaintance with Isabel Kelly, the young anthropologist from the University of California, Berkeley. I met her three daughters, dignified women, generous of spirit, each of distinctive character.

Thelma Sheldon, the eldest, beaded a necklace as thanks for a story I wrote that honored their mother. The character on the necklace is a petroglyph figure she called "little man" that was pecked into a slick rock face in Surprise Valley.

Bea Pollard served with me on a board developed to bring Public Broadcast Television into our valley. The vision realized served us with commercial-free programming, quality shows for all children, as well as thought provoking and informative ones for adults. She wanted those choices for her people.

Juanita McGowan and I were brought together by wild plum jam made from the bitter skinned fruit that grows on tenacious little shrubs in the dry mountain canyons. People have domesticated the shrubs, planting them in their garden spots. But Juanita and I agreed that when taken from their *place*, the taste was not the same. It lacked the wild.

Nellie, Thelma, Bea, and Juanita are all gone now. I am grateful to have known them and other Paiute people of Surprise Valley who, like Lahontan Cutthroat trout, survive in a shrinking world, carrying on their souls the mark of bloodshed. They are the tart fruit that thrives in adversity. They are the prehistoric shrimp burrowed deep into the mud of the playa waiting for water's return.

They are the everlasting cadence of sage. I admire their celebration of their culture through ceremony and daily life as they use humor to make the best of the world that presents itself. They leave behind tokens of kindness, friendship, and their stories.

ONE

# Tokens in an Indian Graveyard

I.

Outside the post office
Wanda Dunn asks, "Who owns
that old cemetery land up Deep Creek?"
Her dark hands work letters and junk
mail into a roll.

"Nobody *owns* the cemetery," I say
of a place not recorded on county maps.
"It's where your people are buried."

"Uh-huh," she says in her Paiute way
ignoring my answer. She twists the mail tighter.
"The Townsends want to fix it up
but they don't want to go on nobody's land."

She no longer thinks of it as her land, too.


II.

I ride my horse up the knoll by Deep Creek.
Over the low barbed wire fence,
among graying wooden markers and stones,
deer have lain.

A purple heart hangs on a nail, a room key
from a Fourth Street motel in Reno,
a graduation tassel - maroon and gold,
a dream catcher to purify the long sleep.
No praying hands carved in marble.

Just tokens
and ribbons floating on the breath of private memory.

1

## The Place Wanda Thinks About

The Groundhog Eaters
came out of the Nevada wind
chalked with alkali

to camp by this creek,
to rest in the shaded grass,
to bathe in water plucking music
from the current.
Men hunted mountain glades
with eyes and ears sharp
for warring bands of the Pit Rivers
and Modocs.

Women's voices echoed
in plum thickets,
on dry side-hills digging epos,
gathering willow wands
to weave baskets, coating some
water-tight with pine pitch.
Children played games of woods
and water.

Wanda said the knoll is a peaceful place.
When time came to gather pinenuts
one hundred miles northeast,
they left their dead behind
buried there, curled in sleep,
facing the Desert.

## Wild Plum Seedling

Small round hands
work up
through tangled grass
to touch the word
Sun.

# Right There!

### Nellie Townsend (c. 1892-1990)

I.

At the old-folks home
Nellie Townsend rolls her wheelchair
toward me.
One leg under a colorful afghan,
the other—missing.

She stops the wheel against my foot.
A hawk's steady eyes behind thick glasses.
(A field mouse anticipates the pierce of talons.)

Patsy Garcia, her friend, draws up a chair,
shuffles papers, aligns edges perfectly.
Patsy's soft voice reassures Nellie
it's just a conversation. Nellie glares
saying something in Paiute.
Patsy blushes and looks my way
(Maybe I understand their native language.)

Nellie spits in perfect English, "If I knew
they was gonna do this
I wouldn't a come out here!"

II.

Patsy begins with an easy question,
"Where were you born, Nellie?"
"You know where!"
Patsy giggles. "Yes, I know where. "
She nods at me helplessly.

Nellie snorts. In a shotgun blast of Paiute,
she pronounces "Cedarville!"
and closes in English - "*Right there!*"

Patsy looks directly into the camera.
"Nellie says, 'In a little clearing in the sagebrush
alongside of Cedar Creek, at what is now Cedarville.'"


III.

Patsy asks,
"Can you sing us a song, Nellie?"

Nellie's stern face melts into a sly smile.
The song begins low and guttural.
Her grin hints that it's a women's song.
Salty. Testy. At the lusty parts
she blushes and giggles into her fist.

Patsy stammers to translate *The Stinkbug song.*
Our laughter joins us on a path of Nellie's life.


IV.

At the Fort Bidwell Indian Fair
Soldiers threw blankets over Indian kids
"to catch 'em and put 'em in school.
They came to my mother's wikiup.
I hid under her skirts
until they went away."


V.

"The men hunted deer, and antelope,
rabbits, ground squirrels, rock chucks, porcupine,

fish, ducks, and geese but they didn't always
catch 'em.
Everyday we went walking
to find rice grass, buck berries, eggs,
pine nuts, or epos to feed them hungry kids."


VI.


"The seclusion wikiup was the place
women birthed their babies. They wrapped
the babies in rabbit skins and
the grandma
made the first cradleboard for the baby.
On the hood she sewed lines for a boy
and diamonds or zigzags for a girl."


VII.


In 1930, Nellie was an interpreter for Isabel Kelly,
an anthropology student
from the University of California.
Isabel was later told—the Fort Bidwell Paiutes
were uncooperative and impossible to work with.
But not knowing of this prejudice
she gathered information.
Her report credited Nellie, her go-between, for success.


VIII.


Knowing the old days were over
Nellie kept at leatherwork, beading,
gathering food, and cooking the old way,
and made her children go to school
to learn the new ways.

IX.

Nellie worked for the white woman
in the ranch house standing exactly
where she saw her first antelope
with soft eyes looking at her.
She—a baby playing
as her mother gathered wormwood and nettle
—looked back at him.
Now she wondered if the antelope
was a young man on a vision quest
or a spirit returned with a message.

The woman said, "Nellie!" in a sharp voice.
She took her eyes off the memory
and followed the brush making soapy circles
on the floor.

When dinnertime came
she took her plate of food outside
under the trees alone.
It began with a table full of hired men
and no empty chair for Nellie.
And it never changed.

She walked her life
from the one-room government housing
to the ranch house of the white woman
where named roses were planted.

Her babies knew the work
of scrubbing floors and clothes
tied to her back
or propped in their cradleboard.

While the men were away
tending cattle on the desert the woman
held hard to the edge of Nellie's plate.
"Take your dinner with me, Nellie."

Nellie looked into the blue eyes,
pulled free from the gripping fingers
and went out where the antelope stood with her
all those years.


X.


Her youngest, Juanita, was sent
to Stewart Indian School in Carson City.
She was so homesick
she ran home again and again.
Authorities sent Juanita to Riverside.
Nellie took her beading basket
and stayed with Juanita for a year
to ease her through the strangeness
until she could stand to stay alone.


XI.


I keep my face without a sign of guilt
for being white,
responsible for their lost way of life
and linked with "the enemy" as all whites are.

I was learning how the Paiute,
outside the "belonging" curve in this valley
belong in the most serene, elemental way
—by virtue of being.
Laughter and stories are their armor
against our white presence.
Like grass in times of drought
they pull to the center and wait for it to pass.
If Nellie could see me cleaning the cemetery
flinging cow pies and pulling tumbleweeds

from the fence wire
her laugh would ruffle the creek below
—a cutthroat trout rolling
just under the surface.

# At The Beginning

First People
prepared to plant
the earth with trees.

The tedious work
sorting the seeds
was nearly finished
when Coyote
came trotting up.

Coyote said,
"I came to help."
They hesitated,
knowing him to be
careless and lazy,

but handed him
a pouch of
juniper berries
and gave him
careful instructions.

"Dig a hole
for each seed
and cover them
well."

"Plant the seeds
far away from other trees.
They are greedy.
They will suck up
all the water,
growing fat
while pine,

willow,
and aspen
will shrivel and die."

"Yes, yes," he called
over his shoulder.

He wasn't even
out of sight
when he gave a laugh,
threw a handful of juniper berries
into his mouth
and spit them out
in a garrulous spray.

Where the seeds landed
a stem sprouted.

Coyote went on
spitting seeds
here and there
as he trotted along
until the bag was
empty.

That is why
young juniper trees
are scattered
all over the desert.

# In the Desert Grove

for Michelle Michel


In carvings
on the bark
in shaded groves

figures
like pollywogs
swimming

signal
a water source

a map
to desert springs.

# Woman's Place

A Paiute woman sat here
where cattails
of worn brown velvet
spawn in the steamy air

to grind pine nuts
gathered with the mountain's blessing
in this lava bowl

that struck my mare's hoof
and led me like a reed whistle
calling widgeon in.

I imagine the rhythm of her body
—rock chewing seeds,

I smell
the pierce of sage
where a magpie grips a branch,
watching.

Did she go to the distant caldera
looking for a stone to shape
—unaware of time
walking toward her—
did she heat it in a greasewood fire
let water beads pop, fracturing flakes,
mere flakes
then chip to form a grinding bowl?

No gentle cove of sand
could stop their wandering
—children strapped to the clutch of women
behind the men—

shoulders hunched toward game or harvest.

Buried in the sand of her home
she left behind heavy stone tools
(metate, mano, mortar, pestle)
her bowl
in this dune of many lives repeated.

## The Racetrack

From the air
a long oval can be seen
cut through brush
by unshod hooves
on the flat hip of the hill.

Those who came before built lodges
and when they got horses
they gathered before winter
hands clenched, boasting,
feeling the hoof-thunder
shake their hearts.

They could not know
how it looked, racing
on that great open mesa
—horses lunging to take the lead,
some spilling blood onto rocks,
shoulder to shoulder, legs tangled,
manes rising in the wind

unless the eagle—he who touches
the beyond and the here—
unless the eagle
told them in a shrill.

## Native Myth

In memory of Clarence DeGarmo

The Serpent
lived in this valley.
He carved a trough along the hills
with his long tail
dropping acid spore
where vents spew steam.

When Lake Surprise drained
down a secret path
he followed it to Pyramid Lake
and from there—no one knows.

Rain came heavy this winter.
The lake filled. I look
for dimples of oil on the stones
and when there is a dark moon
I listen for heavy dragging
of a black and ivory tail
scraping against the gravel bar.

## The Path

In the core
of each cell
patterned into man's being
does he recall
the path he walked
with all the beasts
of earth
and water
and sky ?

And then,
as intellect withered elsewhere
and bloomed in him
to stand upright
and speak,
was that why
he painted
horse
on cave walls ?

Was the promise
in the scripture of his species
to care for those
who did not rise
as he,
to revere his beginnings
recognizing
the wild inscription
in eyes
not unlike
his own ?

I must conclude
he could not go
alone.

Needing freedom
he chose horse
to lift him
and for that
he follows the commandment
made of light

to build a shelter,
harvest feed,
seek their company,
work beside them,
and weep
when they die.

# Mammoth Hunters

In a canyon
not far from where we stand
a petroglyph
scratched into rock

a mammoth
—shock swimming in his eyes,
the blow of a spear
driven deep
through his ribs
impaling his frightened heart

settles the question
of who stalked
the mammoth.

# TWO

# Fort Bidwell Indian School — 1898-1940

*The Fort Bidwell Indian School, located at the north end of Surprise Valley, was established in 1898 in the abandoned United States Army Fort for which the adjacent community was named. The school gave the children of the local Paiute people, as well as children from other tribes, access to education and vocation.*

There came a point of final surrender when the freedom of the Native American gave way to the unstoppable force of the new American. Peaceful sharing of land and resources between the two totally divergent cultures proved impossible. After years of armed conflict, surrender culminated in the enforced confinement of Indians to reservations across the country.

The General Allotment, or Dawes Act of 1887, was seemingly the key to the white vision for the Indian citizen. That legislation made all Indians, including those of the Paiute tribe located in the border triangle area of Oregon, California, and Nevada, into landowners by giving them title to a parcel of land recently wrenched from them. One wonders if the white bureaucracy saw the irony in their "land giving" policy. These Northern Paiutes were less aggressive in their confrontations with the white settlers of their area than the Modoc or the Pit River tribes. They followed the counsel of Chief Ochiho, a Paiute who migrated into Surprise Valley from the war-torn Silver Lake Valley in southern Oregon. He advised his band to stay put in Surprise Valley, and thus avoid the battles of the Modoc and Bannock Wars.

Meanwhile in the East, a different kind of war was being waged. The Paiutes would have called it a "mouth fight." People of advantaged economic and educational backgrounds, some with sincere interest for the well being of the conquered people, and those playing out the benefactor's social concern of the time, formed organizations and groups; representatives of virtually all the religious press; educators; missionaries; and members of the Congress and federal officials were named to the Board of Indian Commission-in 1879, by President Rutherford B. Hayes.

In 1883, Thomas J. Morgan, newly named commissioner of Indian Affairs, brought together the commission that had the strategy for the Indian's future, the political power to impose it, and the naiveté to suppose it would work.

One member, Oregon Indian Superintendent Alfred B. Meacham, spoke with authority on the inequity of government promises and the barbarism of frontier whites. Meacham was himself a survivor of five bullets and an attempted scalping at the Modoc peace talks where General Canby and others were killed by Modocs led by Captain Jack. Meacham lived to become one of the most effective crusaders for Indian rights in the northwest.

In addition to the physical surrender, already a concession, national policy called for the surrender of the Indians' traditional life ways and their language. It was the aim of the commissioners to enact the ideology that a population of 360,000 Native Americans could be absorbed into the "civilized" melting pot of America.

A platform was adopted to bring about the redemption of the Indians by removing from them any trace of their heritage and transforming them into copies of white Christian farmers. The reformers proposed to accomplish the "Americanization" of the American Indian by giving to each man the free ownership in a plot of land and an education to prepare him to become a self-supporting, law abiding citizen. The commission was prepared for swift advancement of their agenda by establishing boarding schools to totally immerse the children in the American ideal of education. The young children would be enrolled by force if necessary and reap the supposed benefits of a new language, new perceptions and goals, and new living habits. The Indians would put aside the old ways and, equipped with the mantle of the whites, would move with ease into the mainstream of social and economic life. This ambitious project was conceived without regard for the opinion of the Indians nor the happy consent of the white society with which they were to blend. The eventuality of the mingling of red and white blood was never addressed.

There was a fourth aim for the reformers: the larger political issue of the dissolution of the Bureau of Indian Affairs to arrest the malignant features of incompetence, corruption, and spoilsmanship already entrenched in the department.

Education was the goal of the commission. In addition to instruction in the English language, emphasis would be placed on vocational training, such as farm and carpentry skills for the boys and housekeeping skills for the girls. Likewise, the schools fostered patriotism – American, not tribal. Commissioner Morgan said,

> *"Teachers should endeavor to awaken reverence for the nation's power, gratitude for its beneficence, pride in its history, and a laudable ambition to contribute to its prosperity. Teachers should carefully avoid any unnecessary reference to the fact that they [the children] are Indians."*

The Department of Interior turned over the military reservation buildings and land for use as an Indian Training School in 1897, but the intended use was indicated on U.S. Army maps as early as 1893.

Both kinds of school systems, the day school and the boarding school, had distinct advantages and were employed at Fort Bidwell. The day school had the benefit of returning the children each evening to a family environment. And the boarding school could more fully involve the students in the vocational program, control the usage of the dominant language, and lessen the influence of family and culture, therefore accomplishing the transition with the least distraction or backslide. The Fort Bidwell School began as a day school, but the boarding school concept was put into effect almost immediately. From 1917 to 1930, local students could live at home or board in. In the fall of 1930 the boarding school was terminated, and only the day school remained until its closure in 1939.

Originally, school was conducted in the former post hospital. By 1900 the converted fort was described as follows:

> The plant consists of superintendent's residence, three
> dwellings (employees), physician's office, sewing room,
> boys' bldg., girls' bldg., laundry and drying room, commisary, carpenter shop, blacksmith shop, gymnasium,
> granary, dairy barn, stable, carriage and implement house,
> girl's bath house, boys' bath house, butcher shop, bakery,
> and a good system of waterworks.

During the years 1900-1906, no buildings were added, although some remodeling and repairs to the water system took place. A fire destroyed the school house in December of 1927. Funds approved by Congress provided a new school house ($26,508) and hospital ($17,164). Under Superintendent Orrin C. Gray (1915-1930), many improvements were made by the additions of a creamery, implement shed, hog shed, dairy barn, and chicken house. The products of these improvements were to provide food for the school and to teach the pupils practical farming techniques.

The initial enrollment of 14 boys and 9 girls was reported in April 1898 by teacher Hylena A. Nickerson. All of the children were Paiutes from the Surprise Valley area.

The method of persuading the parents to allow their children to be taken into the school buildings by whites is open to speculation. The school superintendent was charged with the responsibility of complying with state and federal laws governing compulsory education, even when it meant sending an officer to "abduct" children from their homes. One Indian said, "They came around and picked up our children like you whites pick up dogs, and took them away to school." One woman remembers that when the teachers came to her wickiup to get the children she hid under her mother's skirts until they were gone. Another child hid under a winnowing basket.

The Indian Fair held in Fort Bidwell was used as a method of getting the children into town. Races, rodeo, contests, exhibitions, gambling, and dances attracted Indians from a wide area of Oregon, Nevada, and California. Once in the vicinity, school officers could bring the children to the school. Parents must have understood the benefits of education or they would not have brought the children to the fair where they could be "captured." In later years the students came to recognize the gathering as a sign of summer's end and the return to school. One father said, "If my boy stayed home, maybe he could get a job working for one of the ranchers but if he went to school, maybe he could be a doctor or teacher himself."

Enrollment, which varied over the years, was approximately 100. The majority of the students were split between the Paiutes and the Pit River Indians, but the school was open to all Indian children, drawing mainly from the neighboring states of Oregon and

Nevada. When the Indian school in Greenville burned, the children were sent to Fort Bidwell. During Mr. Gray's tenure, students came from other states because of the reputation of the industrial school and the academic program. In 1926, the breakdown by tribes was as follows: Paiute—73, Pit River—16, Digger—9, Wylackie—4, Konkaw—2, Cherokee—2, Mission—1, and Wintu—1.

In the first years of the school, when the national disciplinary policy was absolute, even cruel, the Indian school was no exception.

Punishments were remembered by students as being severe and painful. There were broken bones. A split leather strap hanging from the wall was taken down for a harsh reminder of infractions of the rules, which ranged from speaking in their forbidden native language, to writing with the left hand, to disobedience. The strap was replaced by the demerit system although there was no evidence of a merit system.

Punishment of one hour of extra work on Saturday afternoon was given for:
  Not saying Grace
  Not making the bed
  Not washing hands and face before meals
  Not keeping in step while marching
  Chewing gum at school
  Being slouchy or dirty
  Forgetting to brush teeth, etc.

The school code included the maximum of ten demerits for:
  Using tobacco in any form
  Stealing
  Immoral conduct
  Desertion

In the eyes of the administration, punishment was justified for individuals who were reluctant to trade enlightened thinking for divergent beliefs, culture, or mores. Those in power felt that the wild nature of the Indians must be squelched and the children brought to heel. Accordingly, there were many desertions. Constables and tracking dogs went after them and sometimes it ended in tragedy. The children were probably not able to recognize that an abrupt collapse in their free-roaming lifestyle had taken place. However, the parents may have grasped the futility of resistance to the power of the whites and encouraged their children to take advantage of the education and training the school could give them. An elder remembers when he was in school he heard a misbehaving white child threatened by his mother with, "I will send you to Fort Bidwell if you don't obey." And another recalls that his own parents said they might have to move to Cedarville if he and his brother didn't stop coming home all of the time.

Conditions in the Indian homes during the first decades of the 1900s were of abject poverty. The native staple, the jack rabbit—considered the Paiute's buffalo—although abundant in neighboring Nevada, was denied to them by restrictive hunting regulations. They were suddenly fined for hunting the deer that roamed the country as they, too, once had. Hard rules, hard laws when a family was hungry. The students must have come to rely on the school's consistent diet. There was enough food to satisfy a child's unending hunger. Women elders who were among those first students spoke of hiding food in their bloomers and sneaking outside to eat because the older girls, who shared their dorm room, left them so little.

The environment of the school changed when Orrin C. Gray was named superintendent. Quick young Indian minds met the academic challenge when they were taught by the competent and kind teachers he hired. In a year-end report, superintendent Gray wrote:

*Over a period of years the average has been over one half continuing beyond the sixth grade course of study maintained at Fort Bidwell Boarding School... The Academic work of the school has been vastly improved this past year. There have been three teachers in place of the two heretofore. The pupils have made rapid progress and in several instances they have made two grades in the one year by doing special work outside of school hours with teachers who have been glad to remain until supper time. There were six pupils starting in the sixth grade in the fall of 1922 and eight finished in the spring of 1923.*

In 1926, he wrote:

*There were nineteen graduates from the sixth grade. Of these, fourteen will enroll in advanced grades of public and Government schools.*

On the subject of teaching the children organized sports with rules and an object to the game, in 1911 he reported:

*The pupils take a decided interest in all up-to-date games such as baseball, basketball and football, and although pitted against the best teams of the valley and the Cedarville High School ball team, have not as yet lost a game.*

When a theater was added to the school, the motion picture found an enthusiastic audience. Cowboy pictures were their favorite, and Hoot Gibson galloping after the outlaws was their hero. Other examples of white society were portrayed for the students in such films as "Abie's Irish Rose," "The Fleet's In," "Sunset Pass," and "The Wolf of Wall Street." Those movie memories of former students, now in their 60's and 70's, are laced with humor, lacking the bitterness that might be expected.

One older man talked about the division of chores among the boys: "The older boys did the heavy farm work, plowing, blacksmithing, machine repair, planting and haying, and working with the livestock. The middle-age boys worked in the garden, the laundry, and did lighter farm work, carrying feed and water to the animals, cleaning the pens, and gathering eggs. The smallest boys were kept inside to help with the housework. They were named the housecats by the older boys. All of the children were taught to keep their clothes clean and mended, and took pride in sewing patches on neatly, so the stitches wouldn't even show."

Illness was inevitable. Flu and childhood diseases were visited upon the Indian school just as they were in the valley population. Tuberculosis was especially virulent among the Indian community. Drs. Kober, Tinsman, Coates, and Coppedge cared for all the people of Modoc County. Their records reflect compassionate, caring professionals who applied their oath equally. The Fort Bidwell Hospital had a capacity of 32 beds in the 1930s. The tuberculosis sanitarium at the hospital was the busiest ward and patients from the entire Sacramento jurisdiction, as well as all of the State of Nevada and southern Oregon, came to Fort Bidwell to enter the sanitarium.

Recognizing the regional agricultural industry, and following the platform set up by the Conference of Indian Affairs, Superintendent Gray developed the industrial school as the focus of the school's influence on the students. He took a struggling vocational farm and put his energy into the modernization of equipment and scientific information. The boys worked alongside the farm instructor, learning as they watched; their labor provided them with harvest and profit. The following are excerpts from his reports:

*The production for the season of 1925 was exceptionally good on the school farm, and likewise on many of the allotments. Considerable early hay was cut before July 1st ...*

*School farm products for the fiscal year 1926 amounted to approximately $8,000 in value [producing] the ample food the children had at school ...*

*Pure blood sires for the dairy herd and the swine herd are kept at the Indian School, and already some very good pigs have been born eligible for registry in the National Duroc Association ...*

*Agency Indians do not as a rule want dairy stock, especially the Holstein breed, being governed in their likes by the great number of Durham and Hereford cattle of the ranchers raising beef strains. It was with considerable pleasure recently that I listened to an Indian School boy working on a ranch during vacation giving the owner some very good pointers on his dairy herd, which like many locally were only milk cows out of his beef cattle stock herd. The owner was sending milk to the creamery and depending upon the income for quite a little of his running expenses. The Indian boy told him he better get dairy cattle, stating the breeds and why, if he wished to make anything financially from his cows.*

*An inventory of farm animals in 1916 was as follows: 7 geldings, 3 mares, 2 mules, 1 registered Durham bull, 19 cows, 12 dairy cows, 11 heifers, 37 steers (1-4 yrs.), 1 boar, 28 hogs, and 78 pigs.*

The administration of the neighboring public school, though friendly to the staff, was not willing to allow the Indian students to enroll in high school due to pressure by white parents. In 1930 the Sacramento Bee ran the following story:

## MODOC SEEKS RETENTION OF INDIAN SCHOOL

Mitchell Tillotson, secretary of the Modoc County Development Board, states that the organization will continue to fight bitterly against the system of transferring the Indian children to white schools throughout the county. [This despite the fact that the Bee reporter continues...] The past few years Indian children have not only made good records in all school work, have out stripped their white brothers and sisters under the guiding hand of Indian service employees.

The financial condition of the Fort Bidwell School improved over the years, and in 1926 Gray sent the following report to his superiors:

*Probably no better summary can be given than to repeat some facts already in statistical form. The income of the Modoc County Indians for the fiscal year ending June 30, 1926 was approximately $100,000. Of this only $5,397 was donated by the government to the Indians for relief, free rations, etc. The total value of crops sold and consumed by Indians including livestock, was $35,000, and wages earned totaled $42,000. The balance of the income was derived from native industries such as basket-making, glove making, sale and leasing of lands.*

Gray was asked by the Paiutes, many of his former students, if they might manage the Fair themselves after a period of time when the whites had let it lapse. He reports:

*The Indian Fair held at Fort Bidwell during the first week of September, 1925, was conducted for the second time entirely by Indians. It was a credit to them and the order maintained was good. As an instance it may be cited that a bootlegger made his appearance the first night about 11 o'clock, and without seeking out the Indian police, he was forcibly ejected from the grounds under orders from the manager, Willie Sam... The exhibits of native industry were exceptionally good and numerous. Judges had difficulty in deciding between three exhibitors for agricultural sweepstakes, and finally called it a tie, awarding a first prize to all three. There was no county fair held this year.*

The Indian Fair ran for three days in the first week of October and advertised many activities: Agricultural and Horticultural Exhibits; Livestock and Poultry Display; Indian Handicrafts, as Baskets, Beadwork, Rawhide and Hair Work; Cookery, Sewing, Gloves, Moccasins, School Class Room Work, Baby Show, Ball Games, Horse Races, Foot Races, Field Sports. In the evening there was a Grand Ball with Music from Alturas, the Rice Orchestra.

The Johnson-O'Malley Act of 1934 started the integration of Indian children into public schools and ended the need for the Indian School in Fort Bidwell. However, the school stayed in operation until 1939, as teachers eased the children into the white world.

In 1938, a Fort Bidwell Indian School teacher, Mrs. Spencer, who was half Cherokee took eight of her students to the World's Fair at Treasure Island. Fifty-two years later, one of the students, the eldest daughter of Nellie Townsend, recollected the journey and the festivities of the World's Fair. Her eyes were bright with memories of what must have been an awe-inspiring adventure for a young girl one generation removed from the nomadic peoples of the Sagebrush corner of California.

By 1940, many of the buildings were dismantled and the materials used for housing and other needs. The ruined remains of other buildings remind us of a time of fear and cruelty, adjustment and learning, courage and encouragement, friendship and pride. Many of the children of that first generation of students at the Fort Bidwell Indian School move easily within the American society of the 21st century. Some are doctors, lawyers, business owners, ranchers, some work in the media, others work for the government. Many are artists and writers. Some continue leather work and the beading traditions of their grandparents and are learning the Paiute language so they can pass on the stories of their people before they are lost. Stories of their emergence are told to the children while the drums beat out a rhythm, and they learn to sing the stories of raven and stink bug, and coyote, and of the animals and plants that gave them life before the white man came. When they lived free.

## House Cats

*Paiute boys too young for heavy work on the school farm were kept in the inside quarters and given easier tasks. The older boys nicknamed them "house cats."*

The Fort Bidwell Indian School,
(1898–1940)

Spit soiled thread
clumsy knots
a sorry copy
of the teacher's example
you sewed buttons
in the upstairs barracks
and where was your mind?

Older boys
worked in the shop's dark file, or
ran from the bay of the constable's dogs
into deep winter ice
crossing sloughs and swamps
to sleep or die
in frozen willow stands.

Older boys
mute
if the split leather strap
was taken from the hook.
In the night they whispered
forbidden Paiute
from their sour bedding
like bats scratching
for a hole to the sky

and the house cats bent over their work
sewing on buttons
—one short thread pulled uneven.

# Redeye

Wagons groan up hill
to the Lake City Flouring Mill.
Horses blow and steam.
Sweat splashes down.

The creek's meager summer flow
lifts the pelton wheel
driving the grinders to make flour.

The millwright tags each sack
unloaded on the dock
with the ranch name.
One sack of wheat for the mill.
Take one sack of flour home.

Out open doors
the mill coughs a fog of pure
white bleached flour.

White women want rolls and cakes
white as snow, biscuits white
and light as snow.
They won't take
the wheat hull and bran called
Redeye

sacked separate,
and left on the dock for whoever
wants it to feed hogs, or
for the Paiutes to take.
*Redeye for Redskins*, they'd say.

Bran and hull – the best
of the valley's hard, red wheat –
cooked up into Redeye mush
making healthy
pigs and Paiute kids.

# A Man Old Enough to Remember the Mahalas

In his small kitchen, wood chips and a hatchet,
ketchup and saltines on the table
he rests his old fist on a week of not shaving.

— We had that 'dobe land around our place
and it growed Indian roots, epos, lots of 'em.
The Indians crushed 'em for flour or boiled 'em,
like potatoes. Wagon after wagon of Indians,
they would come in there to dig 'em, trade 'em
for butter and eggs and pasture for their horses.
Camp right there and have dances at night.
'Course the mahalas had done enough dancin'
on the epos.

The mahalas wore a basket, round on the top,
long and tapering, tied on their shoulders
by buckskin. They used choke cherry sticks
hardened by fire to dig the epos, stooped over,
toss 'em over their shoulder into the basket,
never looked back, pert near all day long.

The little stream that ran through the place'd be
pretty shallow that time of year.
They put a flat willow basket in the creek.
The water'd just skim over the top.
They all wore long skirts in those days.
They'd pull off their moccasins an' lift
their skirts an' barefooted they'd shuffle,
just shuffle with their feet, an' the skimming water
would wash the hulls away downstream.
When they got done the epos'd be just white
and pretty as ivory.

A mahala would dig half a barley sack in a day,
which is a lot of epos. Yes, they'd just shuffle,
shuffle their bare feet an' pick up the ivory.

His crooked fingers rubbed across his face.
The dance, the taste of epos raw,
light sparking on the rippling creek, a curtain of sun
behind the dance, behind his eyes.

*Just shuffle their feet*
*and pick up the Ivory.*

## Woman Talk

"Grandmother said
Paiute women
wore a leather pouch
on a neck string.
They kept sand in it
and when drunk cowboys
came riding into camp
they'd pack theirselves
with sand
so they wouldn't
get raped."

# Homage

In gentle light like this,
the uncut meadow meets me at the gate
in a high uneven beauty.
I begin cutting hay.

On a mid-morning round
a bird's nest rests on top the windrow
as if set down by a breeze.

Moments before, grass swayed
over its brim.
Birdsong trembled the breeze.
A perfect bowl of grass
woven finer and finer until at the inner well
a brighter shade of gold
where eggshell clings.

In gentle light like this,
Paiute women stooped,
turned a nest of perfect weaving
in their hands—to understand the form.
Holding the idea, they wove
green willow strips into a bowl
the size of two cupped hands
learning the increase of youth,
the decrease of years.

Iridescent green feathers of hummingbird,
blue-green of magpie, black-specked yellow
of the meadowlark's throat,
hooked topknot of quail,
woven into the willow pattern
as homage to the teacher.

From the round body of the bird,
round shell, round nest
into a round earth-world,
women know the wholeness,
the unending curve
of constant attention, the security of
nowhere but here.

# Julia DeGarmo

Stands looking at my Bronco,
the rope cinched down,
tying the hood shut.

"Why are you doing that?"

By now we are both chuckling.
I tell her the hinge broke
and the hood flew open.
'I'm waiting for the new part."

Julia shakes her head, smiling
"Looks like a Indian car."


We drive along the valley. Julia
points her chin at a dark blue canyon.
"There...
is where the wind lives."

After a pause she adds,
"Of course, white people
don't believe that."

## Clarence DeGarmo

Steps in front of my Bronco
As I turn the corner
beside the Lowell Store.

"Want to buy
a reeeel gen-u-ine
Indian artifact?"

In a small box, three arrowheads
chipped from dark blue glass.

"I make these from ExLax bottles.
If you shoot a white man
with one a' these
he'll shit himself to death."

I put a dollar into his hand,
and he puts
the blue glitter into mine.

## Hide Trader

Arthur Dunn and I crawl
into the haymow of our old barn
pulling flint deer hides down from the rafters,
cobwebs stringing from our hair, dust.

We stack the hides
stiff and unyielding as tin
in the back of his station wagon.
Arthur rests his hand on the gate.
"I remember your grandfather."

He honors me by the connection
to my husband's grandfather, old man Hussy
of the slaughter plant, of the butcher shops,
of the screen-side delivery truck,
of the missing fingers on his left hand.
"He cut his hand in the meat-grinder, clear to here!"
Arthur's mouth opens in a child's horror
as his finger draws a line across his own hand
straight through his knuckles.
"My mother made him buckskin gloves
for that hand, no fingers, only a thumb."

That same young boy smiles again through his face.
"He always gave us kids wienies.
If he saw us by the road he would stop his truck
and he would say, 'I know you kids is always hungry.
Have some wienies.'"

Arthur will drag the hides from his car,
bury them in damp sand to soften them,
scrape the hair and flesh.

In trade,
Arthur and his wife Avis will tan the hide
and stretch it over a cradleboard frame of willow.
Avis will bead parallel stripes on the shade
for our grandson, born four generations
after the Wienie-man.

# Things You Pick Up at the Post Office

For Dan Mesa


Your dad taught me
to cook steaks, John.
Walter was always there
cookin steaks
for FFA or everywhere.

I helped him at the barbeques.

He told me
when you get the steaks cookin
and the people come up,
ask them
how do you like your steak?

They'll say,
medium or rare or well.
You look the steaks over,
and pick one, it don't matter.
You can give them any one.

But if you ask them,
they go away happy.

## Day Work In Modoc—1971

The flower shop advertised for an imaginative,
talented, co-operative part-time employee.
They hired me instead.

After—here's your station, keep all costs under
50% of value, don't throw away anything
that could be stuck in as filler...—
I was put to work making funeral florals
from boxes of cheap rainbow plastic flowers.

More important, the boss had a routine
that honed his memory skills
or amused him.
At the sound of the bell on the front door
he launched a rapid-fire monologue of gossip
—true, alleged, or made-up—
about the customer winding through tubs of lilies
and glads toward us.
No one was spared. Not even the Father.

I've often thought how different had he called out,

"A-ha, Mrs. Smith, you're looking well today. I read
in the paper the family was home. How nice. Here,
let me pin this darlin' rose on your coat since you're
my first customer this morning! That color was made
for you. Yes, yes. That's right. A free rose.
It's our policy."

Or

"Good morning, Mr. Scott. Missed your valuable input
and vote on the Rotary scholarship question yesterday.
Here, please take this rose home to the Missus. No,

45

it's free. Quite sure. I'd like to. Don't mention it.
It's our policy."

He owned
the only flower shop in the entire county, further —
— for 200 miles in any direction. I figured
He could afford to expand the community chest,
to be the one who made a difference.
OK. I admit it. I've always been an idealist.
In first grade there was a poster I never forgot
—Pin Your Wagon to a Star.
Then why, you might ask,
wasn't I surprised about what happened next ... ?

The phone rang. Boss answered and quickly
wrote out an order, hung up and waving it
announced with dread,
"Jimmie Washoe's wife just died.
The Indians will be coming in to order flowers."

Should we circle the wagons? I wondered.

"We have a policy. Cash only for Indians!
No exceptions! Do you understand?"

(Of course I understood. I lived in Georgia,
Dixie, that's D-I-X-I-E
at the start of the Civil Rights movement....)

"Boss, how'll I know if they're Indians?
When they call up, should I ask,
'Are you a Indian?'
What if they lie?"

I pulled my time card
dropped it in the trash
and like a banana
          I split.

## Working the Grass

The coyote
hangs
still as sunlight
above the golden grass
divining
the tremble of a mole
from the crisp unwrapping
of oat seeds.

Across the ditch
a pair of kestrels
hover,
listening
for insects
in the clover crowns.

Can I hear
another's rapid heart?

# Rhinestone Angel

In memory of Juanita Townsend McGowan

Rhinestone boots on her kitchen counter
she laughed as my wide eyes
lapped over the surprising power
of the glittering stones.

"I found them in a second-hand store,
brand new, the soles weren't even scuffed.

Each time my husband asked me out
I put them on
but when I got to the door
I'd pull them off and put on my shoes.

We'd drive out and I'd see them
sitting on the washing machine,
in the kitchen light.

My husband said, why did you buy them
if you won't wear them? They sure look nice
on your feet, Honey. They'd draw attention.

I'll wear them, I told him.
I'm going to be buried in those boots

and when I get to Heaven
I'll walk up the Golden Stairs
in those rhinestone boots.
Every woman needs a pair
but hardly any get them.
Sometimes you have to buy
your own perfect ride."

# The Un-doing of Heaven's Match

She's returning books
borrowed against the echo of an empty house.
Never read them, I bet. Doesn't taste the coffee
I set before her, doesn't feel
the pick-me-up of its intention.
So deep in the blues.

Husband's gone
from a marriage that took her
from one end of her 30s to the other.

Supper's ready. She says she can't stay.
Red silk blouse says
she's on the hunt of something in town.
But no good time will get close
without a collision on the sorrow she wears.

Grew up on a ranch, married a rancher.
A team going from dark to dark, building a place.
We saw it, the way neighbors do
when there's miles and miles of work between you.

At brandings they snaked calves careful but fast
—God's gift and purely loving to rope.
Head catch with an ocean wave, heel
with a backhand over the hip, a yip and a yowl!
The ground crew timed their look-ups
just to see their dancing loops.

They lived close in a casual way.
Both wore the grease, both wore the pants.
When it came apart
it was like trying to bale up feathers.

He was there for the work
but he'd found himself a town girl,
polish on her nails and time on her hands.

I walked her to her truck.
Before she turned the key she asked the night,
"Wasn't I woman enough for him
or wasn't I enough of a man?"

# Ice Breaker In The Tiki Lounge

For Christina Morgan

Since the divorce
her sister's been hanging at home
with the kids.

She hires a babysitter,
brings her sparkly makeup,
a perfume of discreet allure
drags her to the Tiki Lounge.

They order up a beer and wait
for Mr. Right to drop in.

Paiute guy slides up the bar,
smiling through a Bud Light haze.
He tips his cap back to get
a good look at her.

"You ever gut a deer?
You just stick the knife
in its *ass*
and *rip it*
*up to the head.*

Say,
you're a handsome woman."

# One Paiute, One Not

I.

Two ten-year-old boys
done with roping chickens,
and dogs and men walking by,
roped calves, and talked ropes,
nothing more, just ropes.
One edged ahead, then the other.

Friendship coiled around them
at the home ranch
was left behind with their ropes
at the bus stop.
One was the son of the rancher,
the other, the son of a Paiute cowboy.

After school, walking home,
the air hummed with loops.
In time, two ropes weren't strong enough
to hold them together
and the plain language of the loop
was forgotten.

II.

Thirty years later,
two men in the grocery line.
The rancher is a few dollars short.
The tall Paiute next in line says,
I'll pay the extra.

Thanks, he says. I'll get it back to you
but I don't know your name.

That's all right, the Paiute says,
I know yours.

## One Blade of Grass

There must be a seed
a bit of sweet earth
frost for rest
light rain on a spring afternoon
a leggy ant to cultivate the soil
a killdeer to lay her marbled eggs nearby
so the grass can sway and listen.

# Surprise Valley Is Where, Exactly?

We look up at the sky like we're thinking,
trying to translate the answer
into their urban idea of home.
They look up, too,
expecting to see a star-map.

They say, "I know where Yreka is."
Then, thinking maybe we're deaf
or just old and worthless, they wander off.

Some, with stamina, blurt out,
"What about De-ni-o? Is it close to De-ni-o?"
Our eyes begin to twitch
and we feel unsteady for a moment
—they're getting warmer.

Oh, we used to tell – proudly – about Home,
Corner of paradise. No pollution, No gangs, No crime.
We'd even ask them up to visit.
BAD IDEA. BAD!

They slipped into town towing a U-Haul.
Strange rigs parked in front of the post office.
We heard a guy bought the Jones Place.
'Did he get the grazing permit, too?'
"Naw. He's retiring up here
to raise ostriches and llamas and emus."

We're looking at the beginning of the end.
More houses are going up.
Shops hatch on Main Street over night.
Espresso. Gifts. Antiques. Art.

When settlers stopped
in front of a Paiute wickiup
and asked the man napping on the South side
out of the wind
"Which way to Surprise Valley?"

At first he pretended he didn't speak their language.
When that didn't work
he looked up at the sky in deep thought
and pointed back the way they came.

THREE

## The Story They Tell Is This

On the map you'll see that Andy's Camp is better than fifty-five miles northeast of Surprise Valley, mid-way down Fish Springs Canyon, just below its juncture with Horse Canyon. No one remembers who Andy was, or who his people were, only that he lived completely alone far from the nearest white settlement. He built a small cabin where the canyon widens and fenced the grassy meadow for his horses where the waters of Fish Springs and Horse Canyon join and meander between high canyon walls toward Swan Lake. Sometimes you can step across that creek and not get your boots wet, and sometimes it fills the entire canyon wall-to-wall with grass, and forbs, and clover.

Andy would sit on a stump at his woodpile in the evening and smoke his cigarette and listen for the high cries of cranes passing, and he would watch the light bend against the oncoming night into shadows and hues of surpassing beauty and he was perfectly content.

Andy kept a tidy camp, food enough, shelter, warm blankets, feed for his horses and cattle. But most important was the creek running by his door, for the desert has only one god – Water - and its name is a constant prayer. All life waits for the gathering sigh of its arrival, the feel of its soft entry.

The country south of Fish Springs Mountain drains toward Summit Lake where the Paiutes were encamped, told to stay, never to roam again. (Deny a blue bird the wandering skies. Tie an antelope to a mahogany limb. Tell the Cutthroat trout to stay in the shallows.) When they broke the agreement, troubled men came with guns and drove them back until their impulse to stray nearly faded.

By 1930, Andy was gone from his camp and people were already beginning to forget him. They only remembered his little cabin in the canyon. Other men took over his range and their cattle scattered across the desert. A range rider (We don't know his name.) was working for a ranch owned by wealthy, eastern men, and he was sent out to watch the cattle. He stayed at Andy's Camp. But he was uneasy being alone. He was suspicious of every rider in the distance, every sound, and even of the silence. Meanness, his only defense, made him blind to the pleasure of his own company.

Buckaroos rode out from the headquarters to help the range rider at Andy's Camp gather the cattle, brand the calves, and push them higher on the mountain sides as the feed ripened. One of the riders was a Paiute boy from Summit Lake.

It was said this boy rode a horse with kindness, and that his reata had eyes in the loop. From the first day, the man was hard against the boy. He saw the boy ride as if the horse shared his mind, as if hair the horse shed would cling to the boy and keep him warm. The man felt the heat of jealousy when the jigger-boss sent the boy at dawn - instead of him – to the big corral to rope out day-horses for each rider. The cavyada did not mill to avoid being caught but stood quietly within the rope corral, their tails to the boy as his loop lifted and flew, whispering across the sky to settle on the horse like the hastening of light.

Each horse in the boy's string, day after day, accepted his weight in the stirrup, going forward as if, by coincidence, they wanted the same thing.

The man thought of horses as servants: Forced, if they resisted. Beaten, if they refused. Blood splattered the rowels of his spurs, up the cuff of his pants, and layered thick on the lash of his quirt. He took every chance to brood on how he hated "thievin' Injuns", and sent the boy on the outside circle, "to keep the smell away from civilized folks." In the rodear he pulled a calf uneven for the boy and still the boy's loop would roll down the flank from either side, cup under from right or left, underhand or over, and find the heels. The men cheered the beauty of each catch for the boy was a master of many shots like the culo (the butt) and el viento (the wind).

When the country was rode and the calves branded, the jigger-boss took his men to another part of the range but left the boy behind to help the man dig out springs, scatter bulls, pack salt, and brand as new calves were born.

The man didn't want the boy and said so. The jigger-boss did not care what the man wanted. The boy, without a glance, without a frown, stayed behind at Andy's.

Weeks passed as the man fed himself on envy and hatred for the boy's every virtue. When they left camp, the man would not tell the boy of the job ahead but hooked his horse to gallop, leaving the boy like a dog in the dust. He shirked his part of the camp chores, telling the boy to fetch water and chop firewood. Mealtime, his plate was heaped with hot food; the boy was left to make do with what he left in the pan.

From the first night, the boy pulled off alone. He unrolled his bed on the grass of the horse pasture and, hands behind his head, waited for the muffled approach of the horse band at twilight. They found him, snuffed at his blankets, his hair, his bare arms above the blanket, and slept standing near him or lay in their own constellations under the night sky.

What happened next soaked slowly through time like water through sandstone. It began as gossip and was never denied, words of cuffings, insults, beatings, that the man roped the boy off his horse and dragged him through the brush and rocks until finally, he took the dallies off his horn and threw the rope coiled across the ground to where the loop was tightened around the boy's neck. The boy did not fight back but washed blood off his broken nose, buttoned his shirt collar around the rope burn, and worried a cut lip with his tongue, thinking.

After such a beating, the man rode out of camp alone without a word. The boy stayed in camp and shod his string of horses. The man did not return but the jaded bay, reins dragging, saddle turned under his belly, came up the trail at sundown.

The boy untied the latigo and let the saddle fall. He cleaned the wounds spurs ripped in the horse's belly hide, rubbed dried sweat from him with a barley sack and turned him in the meadow with the cavyada.

After a week or more, the jigger-boss rode in to Andy's to check on things. When he did not see the range rider, he asked where the man had gone, and barked, "Now, don't Injun-up on me. Tell me the truth!"

The boy said the man rode off somewheres, didn't say where he was going. And, he said, he wanted his pay. Then the jigger-boss saw the man's saddle on a fence rail, blanket folded, and he made note of the cuts on the boy's face still healing, the bruised eyes.

Without another word he sent the men out looking, not asking the boy to help, but paid his wage, and watched him go up the canyon toward Summit Lake.

There was a young girl among the folks from town who knew the dangers in the desert of rattlesnakes and badger holes and rode out to search for the man. She said they rode in every direction from Andy's, thinking without saying the man must be dead. She was with the ones who found a little pile of ashes from a fire. Riding abreast to watch for signs, they followed the scrawled trail in the dust to a second, then a third fire where what was left of the body lay, one leg badly shattered. He had crawled more than a mile. It was a grizzly sight for a girl – a man who died of thirst, eye sockets empty, them and his brain pecked out by ravens.

— Eyes that would fly south on black glossy wings high over broken hills and canyons.

— Eyes that would look down on the Paiute village beside a deep-set lake at the base of Summit Lake Mountain.

— Eyes that would watch a boy with a spear, standing on a rock at lake edge waiting for a fish — slashed red at the throat — to surface.

## Cutthroat Trout

Belly
fat with eggs
she
looks up
through
the limits
of her world.

Infinity
changes with the season.

## In 1908

Spoken by Lige Langston

Billy McCluskey
half-breed
half-horse
hired on
with Miller and Lux
at Soldier Meadows
to break horses.

He just stayed right there
at the corrals.
That's all he did was
break horses.
They'd bring him a bunch,
he'd get 'em started
so you could ride 'em.
They'd bring him
a new bunch.
Halter break 'em,
saddle 'em,
get on and off 'em,
so you could do your work.

Range horses.
Wild horses.

'Course they had cowboys
to ride 'em.
I don't think
it would be exaggeratin' a bit
to say he started a thousand horses.

Last time I rode with him
he had that bleedin' ulcer. Heck!
He couldn't eat enough breakfast
to keep a jay-bird alive,
then throw up off his horse
and just ride all day.
I don't know how he did it,
he just did.

# The Staff of Life

Spoken by Pete Crystal

One of the buckaroos
high-graded
a jug of wine
and brought it into camp.
He filled everybody's cup.
He handed one to
Billy McCluskey.

Billy took a big swig
and shuddered,

"Coffee's the staff of life...
but this is better."

## Badger Mountain

Beyond Chinatown
sand, bitterbrush, horse brush, shad scale,
and a shout of hissing
chilled me.

I knew no desert beast
of such an open-mouthed warning
until a four-cornered pillow
raced across the broken ground
toward my horse.

Barely fetlock high,
and yet, it charged.

My horse, all eyes and ears,
and nostrils flared,
met its match
in a badger's dark face
and cape thrown loosely
'round its shoulders.

I spurred away, jumped a bank
as underneath a brush
three small pairs of eyes peered
from a hole
just as she plugged off the light.

# An Unexpected Visitor at the Indian School

For Randy Townsend


Those teachers were strict with us little kids.
No talking. Tend to your work.
One winter day we were practicing penman-
ship when all of the sudden
someone came running down the hall.
It sounded like a herd of horses
stampeding! We didn't know who
was coming to get us
but there was no way out!
Then, the door busted open and in jumped
Santa Claus!
Red Suit, Black Cowboy Boots,
and a Long White Beard made of cotton.
Ho, ho, ho, Merry Christmas!

We didn't know who Santa was.
Never heard of him

I don't think we even knew what
Christmas was.
Santa was hopping around, handing out gifts
and candy from a pillow case.

We were busy sucking candy and holding presents.
No one noticed Santa was gone.
Then we heard him in the next classroom,
Ho, ho, ho Merry Christmas!

Sweet candy and Santa was new to us.
I was grown up before I found out that
Jimmie Washoe was our first Santa.
We thought he was only a buckaroo.

## Neck 'n' Neck

Jimmie Washoe was born
in a sagebrush camp
near Plush, Oregon
about the turn of the century
but that didn't slow *him* down.

Neva Lowell was born in 1894
with a silver spoon in her mouth
but that didn't slow *her* down.

Jimmie grew up small and slight.
Neva was a slip of a girl.

Jimmie half-Paiute, half-Chinese
inscrutable to the second power,
was a feather on a horse's back.

Neva, first woman jockey in the country
wore the finest San Francisco could send.
She didn't need to win to prove her worth.

Ice water in their veins
as they hunkered over horses
racing side by side
urging them to shoot a hole in the wind.
Sometimes her, sometimes him
smiling for the win photo.

One race, they flew, neither giving an inch
around the clubhouse turn, down the stretch.
Neva, pressing Jimmie's horse to the rail
till his stirrup leather broke. He shouted,
"I'm a goner!"
She shouted back

"I hope you break your neck!"
as she left him in the dust.

By 1972, Neva lost her direction.
Her husband died of cancer. Her son's plane
nosed into the Black Rock Desert.

After Neva died Jimmie was the best, no question.
What good is that?

## Jimmie Washoe

Being hospitable, a cowboy at the rodeo
laced Jimmie's coffee with whiskey.
He didn't know until blood twisted
in his stomach. "It poisons me,"
he leans up from the open pickup door,
wiping vomit from his mouth.
His face is ashen. We turn
his big palomino with our saddle horses.

Jimmie rests in the bunkhouse, no strength or hunger.
I carry out soup, tea and raised biscuits.
Beside the path I part the snow where violets uncurl
and place a fingertip bouquet on the tray.
He takes my hand. His eyes reflect a dream.

"At night the horses come to me.
All the horses I've ridden
close around my bed, their long heads nodding,
rubbing against me."

> (Horses at the MC when he was cook's helper, too
> small and weak to ride, hanging on the fence rails
> watching buckaroos in the breaking pen. Horses in
> his string when he could reach the stirrup and do
> a day's work. Horses disappearing into the blizzard
> as they trailed 5000 out-of-feed MC cattle 100
> below-zero miles over Hart Mountain to Frenchglen
> that January in the 1930s. Horses at the P Ranch
> vaqueros – Tebo, Chino and Chico –
> rode with dignity and grace teaching him
> the way of la riata, la jaquima, el freno. Horses
> he rode hard as range deputy after cattle rustlers.
> Racehorses neck-and-neck against that fearless
> woman jockey, Neva Lowell. Horses he gave that
> Apache princess. Horses for his daughter, born
> when he was near 70.)

"All the horses. I know what they want.
I say,    not yet.
They turn and go off, one behind the other.
The last one waits, turns back to me.
I say again,    not yet."

The violets breathe their scent in the air.

## The Only Good Indian

Early in the 1800s, wagons began to crawl
across the deserts of the Great Basin
on shimmering heat
like a string of ants following a deadly sweet trail.

Some took the cut-off north to the Oregon Territory,
others went south down brushy hell-hot ravines
to the Promise of California gold.

Paiute people hid belly-down in the brush
as wagon after wagon passed through
their hunting lands.
Ever on guard, they kept a distance,
watchful of white men slaying deer in the mountains,
of their cattle grazing the country ahead of the wagons,
and the oxen and horses and mules left bloated
with death and rot and flies along the trail.

A Paiute family band camped one fall
in a wide mountain valley
picking plums and elderberries
to dry for winter food.
Just at dusk a group of wagons snaked
out of the basin below,
shuddering over rocks and brush up the valley
toward the Paiute camp.
Around the herd of cattle and horses
the wagons circled, and with lanterns lit,
they glowed in the night like moonrise.

Paiutes on one side hill, white settlers on the other.
        Each family drank from snowmelt streams.
        Each sang at their fires, and told stories.
        Each posted guards.
The night passed in peace.

As morning broke
a cavalry patrol rode into the settler's camp, dismounted
and turned their attention on the Indian camp
high up and across the valley,
where smoke from cook fires threaded through the pines.

The officer said
the soldiers had newly issued repeating rifles
in their scabbards – never yet fired –
polished wood, blued steel, gold-bright shells unmarred.
They were anxious to see how the rifles performed.
He said to the wagon boss, "Now,
what if that rag-tag bunch across the way
was fixin' to launch an attack against you?"

"But they been there all night. They never troubled us none."

"Hypothetical, sir. Strictly hypothetical."
He lowered the barrel of his rifle on the Paiute camp, aimed
at an old man carrying wood, and fired.
The wood spilled from the old man's arms as he fell.

Before the wagon boss could yell out, "Stop!"
the rifles of the soldiers were all-hell-breaking-loose
into the Paiute camp
        target practicing
        fish in a barrel.

Paiute women ran screaming,
        some shot, fallen,
        some covering children with their own bodies. Old ones
        drawing fire from children running, screaming, crying,
        stunned into silent fear.
Bullets split the air like hornets
        past their heads, through their skin,
        through their bones and backs,
        through their arms and legs,
through their hearts and heads,

falling them,
stilling them,
killing them.

The soldiers mounted and advanced on horseback.
No returning fire stopped them killing Paiutes
one after another,
every one they could find,
all.
No need to conserve bullets. It was a training exercise.

A Paiute mother clutching her baby hid beneath
a narrow rock ledge behind a covering of high sage
and bitter brush. But the baby cried of fright
and would not, could not be comforted,
quieted.

The soldiers came closer. She could smell blood
on their bayonets, splattered on their uniforms.
When she feared the baby's shrieks
would lead the soldiers to her
she left the baby and crawled over a small rise
to hide in a brush thicket.

The shooting was one slow pop! after another
until silence lay on the mountain as chill and thick as fog.
The settlers pulled out.
The soldiers rooted like pigs through the camp
for survivors,
for souvenirs.

In a thicket high on the hill
the woman's sister
caught up with her.
Both had bleeding wounds, gashes, torn clothing.
The sister asked,
Where is your baby?

I left him behind! the mother wept.
He wouldn't stop crying.
I was afraid they would find us and kill me, too.
I left him behind! she screamed, beating herself
and scratching her own face bloody
       in agony
       sorrow
       shame.

The sister slipped the basket straps from her shoulders,
let the basket to the ground,
and from under a rabbit skin blanket,
       drew out the baby
her sister left behind.

The soldiers were running at me. I heard
your baby cry deep under the ledge.
When he felt my body, he stopped crying.
The soldiers didn't find me!

The sisters clasped each other around the baby
       and wept their relief
       and sealed their hatred of the white invaders.

The officer reported the incident to his superiors.
To account for the ammunition spent
he said, "An engagement was forced
       to save white settlers
       from massacre by Paiute killers."

The settlers packed the murderous attack
on the Paiute families
by the officer and soldiers
with them on the Oregon Trail.

The U.S. Army took no punitive action.

That baby was Jimmie Washoe's grandfather.

# A Friend Spoke At Jimmie Washoe's Graveside

Jimmie came up and stayed with me,
more as he got older.
He'd get cranky and Marie'd call,
"Come and get him!"
He and I talked about old days, old friends.
I took him places he wanted to see again.
We were going over Hart Mountain one day
when an antelope came running hard
right at the car and, boom! he smacked
right into the side of it and fell over dead.
I figured I might just as well cut its throat,
at least save the meat
but the antelope woke up.
And he was on the fight!
I was on the wrong end of a mad
antelope! If I let go he was going to work me over
with his horns. Just then Jimmie
came running with the tire iron
and, boom! he killed the antelope.
Then,
He threw his hands in the air, dancing
—half Chinese fireworks—half Paiute War Lord,
screaming, "Wild Meat for Wild Men!"

They shouldn't have buried Jimmie in the ground.
They should have done like Plains Indians
and put him up in the air
where we can all feel him.
Never was a man so alive.

## The Weir

Tonight I open the ditch through the calf lot.
Ice breaks into puzzle pieces
That will freeze down
—never again with this smooth skin.

Calves stand at a distance watching.
Them freshly weaned and curious.
My head down, busy.

When my shovel goes in
dark ground breaks open
with bright pink water
as the lowering sun
lays one thin finger on my work.

It's quiet.
Geese are already bedded on the lake.
The sky is wide and empty and full.

Calves crowd up behind me
—red light, green light—
sniffing puffs of sweet oats
on my back, in my hair.

There's a rustle overhead
in winter branches.
A hawk draws in long wings.
Bare limbs bloom other hawks.
One is white
but rouged with the same sunset
that fills my small ditch.

FOUR

## Burk, Edsel, Jimmy, and Arthur Brown

For the Brown kids
the path
from the Cedarville Rancheria
to the elementary school
took a short-cut
through Hussa's yard
to Johnny's sand pile
with trucks and a loader,
bicycle and wagon,
cap gun and cowboy hat,
baseball and bat,
cookies and Kool-aid,
swing in the apricot tree.

If Johnny wasn't home
they found him next door
at his grandma's
who wiped their runny noses,
stuffed tissues in their pockets
and sent them back out to play.

## Class Reunion

Burk was the Paiute action hero.
When Johnny complained about
having to wear suspenders
Burk threw them under the lawn mower
and lickety-split
cut them into a million pieces.
It was Burk's idea to hang the outlaw from a limb.
Johnny's mom took the rope away.
Burk said, "Go ask your mom for more cookies,
Johnny Hussa."
"Go sack your head, Burk," Johnny said.

The line between right and wrong
wavered for Burk.
In high school it disappeared altogether
when he got caught stealing money
from the Hornet Annual fund.

Ten years later
it was Burk calling at three in the morning
from Wickenburg Arizona to say, "Johnny Hussa,
my car broke down. I need money to get it fixed.
I got kids and no food for them.
You can wire money to this post office box 114."

The empty phone buzzed in John's hand
like a rattlesnake. I started the fire and made
coffee for anti-venom. He drank it down and said,
"Something's not right. I don't want to leave a guy
stranded but," shaking his head, "something's
not right."

When it got light, he called another classmate.
Funny thing, he got the same call.

The phone was busy all morning.
Everybody in their class got Burk's SOS.
The one who was a lawyer called
the sheriff in Wickenburg.
Sheriff called back. It was a drug drop.

Burk was the outlaw
hanging from the limb.

# Counting Coup

I.

While Burk and Edsel and Jimmy
were in the front yard
running over Johnny's suspenders
with the lawn mower
Johnny's mom Kay was on the back
stoop cutting the Brown girls' hair.
Kay worked in a real beauty shop
but on her day off
when the girls needed haircuts
they'd take turns sitting on her step stool.
Their youngest brother Arthur
would sit and watch her part off some hair,
snip, snip, part off the next bunch, snip, snip
until all the hair would curve in one thick
layer of smooth, shining black.


II.

Arthur learned to cut hair like Kay later on.
It was a job he could do after Viet Nam,
after Agent Orange spewed out of the sky
searing all the leaves of bamboo and him
and his buddies. It was explained as a
tactical error like friendly-fire
but the soldiers were too sick just then
to hear about mistakes.

He had headaches after he left the hospital.
He could only see shafts of light
like night patrol when flares shot up
and came down followed by bursts of gunfire
in the Mekong Delta dark.

Arthur wore dark glasses all the time
and concentrated on the thin bit he could see.
He learned to cut by the feel of hair curled
round his brown fingers.
But he never talked about it
in his little one-man shop in town.


III.


One guy
from Arthur's high school class
took his little boy in for a hair cut.
When somebody said,
"Say, Tommy,
where'd you get that neat haircut?'
the little boy gave a sober reply,
"From a blind Indian."

I guess Tommy knew what we didn't.


IV.


Kay cut her husband's hair only once
right after their wedding.
Ever-after she refused, complaining
Walter's hair was like a porcupine's.
Each snip of the shears sent hair flying
to shatter and shower all around the room
like bits of glass or wire.
She found his hair stuck in the butter,
in her sourdough crock, inside her mind.

V.

Lately,
Arthur's eyes have been getting worse.
Last time John took Walter by Arthur's shop
the magazines were stacked up neat on the table.
No one sat in Arthur's chair.
No Arthur either.
The barber pole wasn't turning.
An arrow pierced the word, Closed.
Walter said,
"I guess, Arthur's done taking scalps."


IV.

"You've gone through everybody else, Dad,
Let's go home and get out the sheep shears."
John turned Walter's wheelchair around
and pushed his father back to the car.

## Drawing Names

I.

In Surprise Valley – second grade
kids drew names for Christmas
by reaching into a pickle jar
and pulling out a folded piece of paper.

Maxine Pete drew Johnny Hussa's name.
Her eyes were still
as Mrs. Hill wrote in her book
and the next row came up jostling,
pushing each other.

Even on cold days, the Brown kids ran
past Maxine's house after school
to Johnny's. By the window
she sewed new dresses for her storybook doll
or beads on leather

and wished to go across the school yard
to swing or play tag with the kids.
But Polio had twisted her leg.
She moved like a broken toy.

II.

As Christmas drew near the kids
piled into T. H. Johnstone Co. who advertised
      "Santa left a big load of toys
      and nice things for girls and boys...."
They bought marbles with agate shooters,
yoyos, comic books, hankies or jacks.
Cassie Johnstone and Billy Fenwick

didn't care if they filled the store with noise.
Cassie wrapped their gifts, and Billy
led them to the row of candy jars
and let them each choose a piece

When they left, it was ungodly quiet again.


III.


Maxine's father left the house at dawn,
a 30.30 in the crook of his arm. He followed
a deer track pressed in the fresh snow toward the old cemetery.
At the fence, he stopped
though the deer's tracks dug deep
where it landed soundlessly among the graves

and out on the other side. Quickly
he ran up the steep hillside, pausing
where he could look down on the trail
just as the deer crossed the creek
and lay down beneath a rock ledge,
becoming one with blue clay, black lava rim,
pearl gray clouds low in the sky.

The rifle's thump echoed in the canyon.
The deer pitched forward, rolling, caught
by an antler against a small pine,
its head lolled back, blood oozing
thick and red

gushed and splashed his hands
when he cut the throat and his knife
whispered up the belly. Guts rolled out
in steaming coils and royal purple organs.

The deer hanging in the shed
would feed his family through winter
but the hide, peeled and soaking in the creek,
was for a pair of buckskin gloves
for Johnny.


IV.


In the window of Kober's store
across from T.H. Johnstone's
Johnny loitered, looking at
buckskin gloves hung on a string.
One size, for men only.

Buckaroos bought them,
and wore them folded inside
the waist band of their pants
when they were in town.
Buckskin gloves
were part of their gear
like a silver bit or spurs.

Looking at them hanging there,
wanting a pair,
did not make them small enough
for a boy's hands
—even a boy who
wanted to be a buckaroo,
someday.


V.


When the hair on the hide slipped,
Maxine's father dragged it over a log,
and with a sharpened bone,
scraped hair and flesh
into piles around his wet shoes.

Maxine's mother smeared the brains
on the flesh side. She pulled
and stretched the hide again and again
as it dried until it was soft.
This was a job most men would not do
—the rotten smelling hide and the hard work
took many days of wetting and stretching
to loosen the fibers.
This hide was cured by a woman's hand alone.

She dragged the hide over a frame of green sticks
and a fire of dozy juniper, and moss
until it smoked deep yellow.

Maxine's hand was her mother's pattern.
At the cuff she sewed diagonal rows
of blue and black beads.


VI.

Johnny wore Maxine's Christmas gloves
even when the hired men teased him,
calling him Injun brave,
and laughing loud
that he was holding hands with
his little squaw.

Maxine protected him from rope burns
as he learned to take his dallies,
and from the cold, and like the men,
he tucked his gloves in the waist of his pants
when they weren't needed.
After they wore out
the drift of branding smoke
and the wink of sparks in the firelight
brought her near.

VII.

The day Johnny turned 21
he went into the Cedar Lodge to buy a beer.
Lively music met him at the door.
Down the bar sitting with her father
was Maxine Pete.

She moved away in third grade.
Arthur said she had an operation
to fix her leg, to keep her body
from lurching with each step.
Now there was no limp.

But, old enough for war,
old enough to vote, old enough
to drink legal, Patsy Cline on the jukebox
singing, *Crazy*, and
—even with Maxine's beauty
on the tip of his tongue—
Johnny could not ask her to dance.

## Imago

A doe drinks
at the edge of a creek
in the shade of the canyon.
Beyond,
where the creek goes
underground
to raise further on,

does her reflection
carry with the water
rushing to surface again
floating
like a sheen of oil?

FIVE

There were no other travelers on the mountain pass. John's truck dragged the stock trailer up the west side in six inches of swirling snow that had fallen since the plow passed over. He dug his watch from under his cuff and tipped it in the dash light. Quarter to one. Almost five hours, fighting this storm. The slip of tires on ice knotted his stomach. He worked to keep the truck on the road by sheer will.

Near the summit, the wall of the storm turned his headlights back into his face, splaying them out in a brilliant glare, consuming them into whiteness. He stared blindly into the snow sweeping off the sheer sided cut, thumping against the truck, fishtailing the trailer. Gusts shortened visibility to mere feet. He geared down and crept forward knowing that once he topped out, the corkscrew-turns on steep grades led to straight stretches that would take a fool on a fast ride.

He'd been the fool in his youth, driving too fast, passing on blind turns. But the mountain chose to let him go, and let him learn by following the tow-truck, ambulance, and cops up the grade to pull people out of cars gone over the edge. In his senior year, the Driver's Ed. instructor loaded the student body on the buses and made them stand where two black tracks suddenly left the earth. Most of the girls stood back, their arms drawn around their bodies as armor against what they knew was below. But the young warriors walked to the edge and looked down at the fire blackened twist of metal mostly hidden by the rip-rap of highway fill and burned brush at the base of the cliff. The night before, while they were watching Rawhide on TV or talking on the phone, men had gone down on ropes and carried two bodies up the rocky slope to the road exactly where they stood, the bodies of two brothers who lived in a dinky travel trailer behind the elementary school with their power-line crew-boss father. Didn't have any friends. Didn't want any. Bragged they'd lived in Denver, and Boise, and Santa Fe, and thumbed their noses at our small-potatoes valley, said they couldn't wait to get out. Now, they weren't going anyplace.

John called from Reno and said he was coming on home. And I wanted him home, but my good sense told him to stay put until the storm blew by. I shifted the phone on my shoulder and turned the TV down. The weatherman's arm followed the counter-clockwise flow of the front that obliterated the map.

Listen, I'll take you a day late and in one piece.

Don't worry. I got a sandwich and coffee. You know how these storms can hit or miss. If it gets too bad, I'll pull over. I've got my bedroll and Buffy to keep the bad guys away.

Buffy wouldn't bite anybody.

Heck, too. She's an A-number one watchdog, I tell you. She growled at the pump jockey when I fueled up. Say! I sold the mare. I'm bringing a turkey, a jug of wine and a present for my Sun-shine.

I wish you had sunshine instead of snow.


The mountain fought against the storm shaking its shaggy mane, tumbling snow from branches as the truck started down the road in its slinging, graceless turns. At that moment, when he forgot to breathe, to hear nothing but the pounding of the storm, in that deeper silence the wind bayed up a vision. A form folded between waves of treachery and the ebb of wind, crusted white in the pin-point of headlights, leaning into the pitch of the driving snow, then suddenly lifted by hanks of long black hair in dark wings above her head as if the squealing wind meant to draw her up whole into its passion.

It was all he could do not to slam his foot on the brake. He eased toward the shoulder and let the truck roll to a stop. Wind tore the door from his hand and sucked the air from his lungs. He struggled against it, as if in harness, toward her. She did not see the truck, the lights, or him coming toward her. As he reached out, she collapsed into his arms.

Flashlight, thermos, dog shoved across the seat, heater flipped on high, he slid her in and ran to the other side. Her body began to shake violently as cold and heat battled for a hearth within. She was creek rocks encased in ice, sheen over the surface of stone. She was snow crystals swelled on fence wire and weeds and in the veins of leaves. She was the breath of horses frozen on their own whiskers. Slowly, the ice began to melt into an Indian woman.

In compound low, he eased the truck down the mountain winding along the deep body of the canyon. Rocks strew the road in places where the wind sucked downward. A doe and fawns lifted their heads from the salt plowed on the road edge, and froze in the sudden light as the truck and trailer went by. In the narrow canyon walls of wind channeled downward gaining velocity, rocking the truck. A few more miles brought them deeper into the narrows where the canyon opened abruptly to the gaudy dance of colored lights. Motel first, then houses, Main Street further ahead.

He watched her silent body wanting to know what she was doing out in this storm, why she was walking. But he asked nothing. She was nearly unconscious, slumped against the door. Being inside the truck out of the storm gave her a chance to turn back from death.

As they passed the Rancheria, her eyes opened on a handful of houses and locked on a snowbound black Galaxy parked in front of one of them.

Do you want me to take you somewhere?
She shook her head no, teeth hammering.
Hospital?
No, again.
We've got a bunkhouse, you can stay there tonight. Figure out tomorrow, tomorrow. That okay?
She looked at him, hesitating, then nodded.
Was I ... almost ... to ... Alturas?
God, no! You were short by twenty miles.
He felt her reaction more than he saw it as the shattering of ice. She was not prepared for that truth.

I heard him open the kitchen door. Crouched beside the bed, his face was stiff with cold and lined with fatigue. My hands on his skin felt like fire.

Honey, I brought someone home. A woman. She was walking up the pass and she's damned near froze. I put her in the bunkhouse. I think she'd feel better if she could see you. Could you get up and come out there? I'm goin' out and get a fire started. Her name is

Diane. I think she's pregnant.

She was the coldest upright person I'd ever seen. The only thing close was in every casket at every funeral, that putty gray of blood drawn off, the stupor of having lost track of life. I handed her a cup of coffee and pulled the rocker near the fire.

Sorry. It's leftover. Might be pretty strong.

She wrapped both hands around the mug and hugged it to her chest. A thin poplin raincoat, just one layer over a knit dress and canvas shoes between her and the storm that tossed the rose bush scratching outside the window. I turned the electric blanket on high and draped a wool robe around her shoulders.

Can we call anyone? Do anything? I can call Dr. Roberts, if you want?

No.

I think she shook her head. Her body was working to get her blood moving.

Take a hot shower. Long as you want. Get some sleep. If you need anything, we're right across the yard. We'll see you in the morning.

What happens to a baby when hypothermia takes over the organism that is the mother? Does the mother suffer the extreme of all her energy drawn to heat her core where the fetus floats? Or is some held back to protect the mother because without her, the baby couldn't stay alive. We talked that over lying close together in our bed. Diane is the product of centuries of survival of the fittest, John mumbled before he fell into the warmth of sleep. That was the only relief he could gather and hold.

A golden plume of light danced out and back across the linoleum toward her feet. She was looking at the picture hanging above the stove as it used to hang in John's grandfather's meat market. A cheap print, familiar in many ranch houses, filled with melancholy. A lone wolf in the winter cold looks over his shoulder at a settler's cabin. Smoke trails from the chimney and a shaft of lamplight at each window reaches into the deep blue night of the wolf's domain. It is loneliness and regret; it must be how Diane's people looked back at those who pushed them out of their country. People like us.

Grandmother had a chair by the fire. Grandmother held her curled even when her legs grew long and their heads touched. She rocked between flick of the fire, Grandmother's stories, dance of fire, warm body of Grandmother. Cedar smoke blessed Night Walking Woman. She spoke to the unborn child cradled by her hands and asked forgiveness. Corn pollen gathered for the birth blessing in a beaded pouch hung between her breasts.

Firelight on the ceiling became her man's face twisted by the collapse of ashes, twisted by a night of tequila and beer. The party was loud and hot. His friends were strangers to her. In their company he was also a stranger. When it was time for the giveaway, a thin woman handed her a package. It was a feathered roach clip.

My baby don't do drugs, he said. But she can use it for a diaper pin. Or I can make good use of it, he laughed.

She whispered again, Let's go. It's a long drive over the mountain and the snow. Please.

He smiled, walked her to the door. His fingers were soft on her arm. He helped her into her coat, opened the door and pushed her gently out onto the porch. He turned back to them as he closed the door.

Christmas tree lights blinked a smear of color through the window. Santa swung from a tack on the door. She snapped the roach clip on his coal black boot.

No keys in the car. She pulled her coat tight. The heat of the house left her body. She started walking and looked back at the house.

Please come after me.

House after house. All is calm. All is bright. The power station. The bulk plant. The mill. Last of the houses. The dark canyon opened like a doorway. Snow flakes reeled with her longing to be a child nestled all snug in her bed.

Please come after me.

She hid in the trees when a car went past. Another. Then a truck. Headlights bent through turns, behind the breast of rock. None were his car. Snow burned on her face. She held her breath when the mountains echoed her name. In the space between snow clouds and her eyes, she heard her grandmother beckoning, and continued up the mountain pass.

Morning is ten below zero and clear. The storm is gone. Cattle watch John load hay on the wagon from the stacks. Frost shimmers on their backs in the slant of sunrise. Their breath is fog around them, trailing off into blue sky.

The TV weatherman, same suit, different tie, pushes the dense white system toward Utah with his hand and magically the storm obeys. I'm taking biscuits out of the oven when he comes in with an armload of wood.

She's awake. The light's on. Should I go get her?

Sure. Breakfast is ready. She ought to eat something. Try not to sound too cheery.

Diane is next to me in the truck. John drives. She sat quietly while he ate his breakfast and then told us she wanted to go home. Her quiet deepens as we pass the Rancheria. The car is gone. Where is Party Man? Driving the roads in desperation? Leading a search? Telling his story to the cops over again?

Every turn of the mountain road is a greeting card. Pine boughs sway like iced trees around gingerbread houses. The placid beauty of deep snow in the forest and mists blowing off the peaks unsettles me. The danger of the night before disappeared so completely. Every mile we climb adds to the weight on Diane. She says she didn't remember it being so far. Didn't remember the mountain so high. Didn't know the country. She is Navajo, from Arizona.

Kids are sledding on the ski hill. The skiers won't kick them off till the tow starts at noon. All angles of arms and legs and bodies slinging down, climbing up again. Coats and caps and shining sleds. From the ridge across you could pick out your kid—their voices, high, joyful like bells.

Near the summit, John says, This is where I picked you up.

She barely breathes, Was I almost there? She forgets she had already asked him that or now that she has seen the mountain and the distance and the depth of the snow, she wants a different answer.

No, he says without looking at her.

From the summit of Cedar Pass a hundred miles across the Modoc Plateau to the west, Mount Shasta stands up in perfect mountain majesty. No storms coming, as far as we can see. The blizzard Diane walked into the night before passed by in a few hours.

In a dozen more miles, John turns at the Chimney Rock Road and enters the upper Pit River Rancheria. A Galaxy is parked beside a white cottage in the small gathering of cottages. John stops, turns the truck off. No one comes to the door.

Diane gets out, walks around to John's door. He gets out. She embraces him and looking directly into his eyes, says,

You saved my life. My baby's life.

She walks across the yard and goes in without looking back.

And now I understand the meaning of last night.

For all the sorrow there has been between our people, we are human beings, after all, and we will watch out for each other.

# The First Camp McGarry

On the shores of Summit Lake
the U.S. Army built a camp in 1866.
Ruins of the barracks, barn, parade ground.

The officer's quarters
had a fireplace in each end.
It was only occupied one year
—too cold beside the lake.
The layout is in the Army archives.
They keep records of everything except
                blood spilled,
                sorrow, pain
                death.

Summit Lake reflects the cries
                of children and women starving
                and freezing
                after their men were killed.

As we walk to the soldier camp
pickup trucks and Paiutes
throw up dust of spinning tires
and questions.

                Who gave *you* permission?
                What do *you* want?
                Who are *you*?

A Paiute woman steps forward.
John says, "Newt?"
She giggles and hugs us.
The dust settles.

In our daughter's High School Rodeo days
Newt came to Cedarville for the rodeo.
Katie invited Newt to stay over with her
　　　　—daisy wallpaper, stereo rockin',
　　　　pretty little girls
　　　　puttin' on war paint
　　　　for the rodeo dance.

That was a long time ago.
But we didn't forget.
Newt didn't forget.


II.


With any luck we will realize
all the things we lost
and all the things we could have learned

　　　　if we just sat quietly
　　　　with the people on these pages
　　　　—these and others.

Maybe our way
wasn't the best

　　　　after all.

Balance is critical—
　　　　for every new idea
　　　　you must make room

　　　　give up unkindness,
　　　　distrust, impatience,
　　　　judgment.

　　Let's start now.
　　　　　　Let's start now.
　　　　　　　　　Let's start now.

# The Author

L INDA HUSSA lives in Surprise Valley, near the small town of Cedarville in northeastern California. She and her husband John, a third-generation rancher in their valley, raise cattle, sheep, horses, and the hay to feed them.

Linda has published four books of poetry, a biography of a Nevada buckaroo, *Lige Langston: Sweet Iron;* short stories, articles, and essays, and along with two other women, wrote about her life and concerns in *Sharing Fencelines: Three Friends Write from Nevada's Sagebrush Corner.* Her book *Blood Sister, I Am To These Fields*, published by the Black Rock Press in 2002, won the Western Heritage Award, the Western Writers of America award, and the Women Writing the West award as best poetry book of the year. In 1999 she received the Nevada Writer's Hall of Fame's Silver Pen Award and she has been a featured poet at the Cowboy Poetry Gathering held annually in Elko, Nevada.

*Colophon*

Designed and produced by Robert Blesse at the Black Rock
Press, School of the Arts, University of Nevada, Reno.
The typeface is Californian, which was designed by
Frederic W. Goudy in 1938 as University Old Style,
an exclusive typeface for the University of California.
Printed by Thomson-Shore, Dexter, Michigan.

BLACK ROCK PRESS